Lerner SPORTS

SPORTS VIPs

MEET TREVOR LAWRENCE

DAVID STABLER

Lerner Publications ◆ Minneapolis

Lerner Publications Company
An imprint of Lerner Publishing Group, Inc.
241 First Avenue North
Minneapolis, MN 55401 USA

For reading levels and more information, look up this title at www.lernerbooks.com.

Main body text set in Aptifer Slab LT Pro. Typeface provided by Linotype AG.

Editor: Cole Nelson

Library of Congress Cataloging-in-Publication Data

Names: Stabler, David, author.
Title: Meet Trevor Lawrence : Jacksonville Jaguars superstar / David Stabler.
Description: Minneapolis, MN : Lerner Publications, [2024] | Series: Lerner sports. Sports VIPs ; 01 | Includes bibliographical references and index. | Audience: Ages 7–11 years | Audience: Grades 4–6 | Summary: "Trevor Lawrence, the first overall pick in the 2021 NFL Draft, is one of the most exciting quarterbacks in the league. Follow his story from childhood to the college national championship and beyond"— Provided by publisher.
Identifiers: LCCN 2023019213 (print) | LCCN 2023019214 (ebook) | ISBN 9798765610480 (lib. bdg.) | ISBN 9798765623664 (pbk) | ISBN 9798765618066 (epub)
Subjects: LCSH: Lawrence, Trevor, 1999—-Juvenile literature. | Quarterbacks (Football)—United States—Biography—Juvenile literature. | Football players—United States—Biography—Juvenile literature. | Jacksonville Jaguars (Football team)—History—Juvenile literature.
Classification: LCC GV939.L368 S83 2024 (print) | LCC GV939.L368 (ebook) | DDC 796.332092 [B]—dc23/eng/20230518

LC record available at https://lccn.loc.gov/2023019213
LC ebook record available at https://lccn.loc.gov/2023019214

Manufactured in the United States of America
1-1009638-51721-7/26/2023

TABLE OF CONTENTS

COMEBACK KID

In January of 2023, the Jacksonville Jaguars played their first National Football League (NFL) playoff game in five years. They were facing off against the Los Angeles Chargers. The Jaguars believed their second-year quarterback, Trevor Lawrence, would lead them to a win. But at first, it looked as if that might be a mistake.

Lawrence struggled at the start of the game. He threw four interceptions in the first half. The Jaguars fell behind 27–0. But Lawrence refused to give up. Just before the half, Lawrence threw a pass to tight end Evan Engram for a touchdown. After a successful kick from Riley Patterson, the score was 27–7.

FAST FACTS

DATE OF BIRTH: October 6, 1999
POSITION: quarterback
LEAGUE: NFL

PROFESSIONAL HIGHLIGHTS: threw three touchdowns in his first NFL game; was the number one overall pick in the NFL Draft (2021); led the Jaguars to a division title (2022)

PERSONAL HIGHLIGHTS: led an undefeated season in his rookie year at Clemson (2018); was a finalist for the Heisman Trophy (2020); married his high school sweetheart, Marissa Mowry (2021)

Trevor Lawrence throws a pass in a 2023 game against the Los Angeles Chargers.

In the second half, Lawrence came out ready to win. On Jacksonville's first three drives, he threw touchdown passes to three different receivers. After the third score, Lawrence ran the ball in from the one-yard line for a two-point conversion. This closed the gap to only two points. The Chargers led 30–28.

With the game on the line and five minutes left to play, Lawrence led a drive to set up a field goal. As the clock ticked down to zero, Patterson sent the ball through the goalposts. The Jaguars won 31–30. The crowd went wild. Lawrence was the NFL's newest comeback kid. But where did he come from?

Lawrence celebrates after the Jaguars win against the Chargers.

CHAPTER 1

HOT PROSPECT

William Trevor Lawrence was born on October 6, 1999, to Jeremy and Amanda Lawrence. His family called him Trevor. He has an older brother, Chase, and a younger sister, Olivia. His family moved to Cartersville, Georgia, when Trevor was five years old.

As a boy, Trevor was known for being a gifted athlete but a clumsy kid. He loved to play football, baseball, and basketball in the backyard with his friends. But he was also known for tripping over his shoelaces on a regular basis. By the time he reached eighth grade, Trevor had outgrown his clumsiness and settled on football as his favorite sport.

Trevor Lawrence playing for the Cartersville Purple Hurricanes in high school

In 2013, Trevor hoped he would have a chance to make the Cartersville High School football team. Head coach Joey King had a rule about not letting eighth graders on his practice squad. But after meeting Trevor, he decided to give him a chance. It didn't hurt that Trevor was tall for his age. He was already 6 foot 2 (1.9 m).

Lawrence warms up before a 2015 game.

SUPER SPORTS SCOOP

Lawrence is known for his long hair. But he didn't start growing it out until his freshman year of high school. Before that, he wore a super-short buzz cut.

During one of his first practices, Trevor picked up a fumbled ball. He leaped in the air and threw the ball straight into the arms of a wide receiver down the field. "Whoa," Coach King said after the game. "This kid is going to be special."

Trevor soon moved from the practice squad to team games. He became the starting quarterback in ninth grade. In his time at Cartersville, he led the team to a 52–2 record, including 41 straight wins and two state titles. He also broke the Georgia state record for passing yards and passing touchdowns.

Trevor's skill caught the attention of colleges across the country. More than 100 college coaches visited Cartersville to watch him play. Once there were so many people lined up to meet him after a game that Trevor had to sneak out the back gate to avoid them.

Lawrence running the football

Lawrence passing the ball in the 2021 Sugar Bowl

When it came time to pick a college, Trevor chose Clemson University in South Carolina. The Clemson Tigers played close to his home in Georgia and had an outstanding football team. With the nation's top up-and-coming quarterback joining them, they set their sights on winning a national title.

CHAPTER 2

COLLEGE SUPERSTAR

In the fall of 2018, Trevor Lawrence began attending classes at Clemson University. When the football season began, he was the team's backup quarterback. But after just four games, his coach put Lawrence in the starting position.

With Lawrence leading the offense, the Clemson Tigers enjoyed a historic undefeated season. They went 13–0 to earn a spot in the national College Football Playoff. In the opening round, Clemson defeated Notre Dame. Then they played for the championship against the Alabama Crimson Tide.

Lawrence ran for 943 yards in three seasons at Clemson.

Lawrence passing the ball in the 2019 College Football Playoff National Championship

Alabama was favored to win. They had won six of the past nine championship games. But Clemson shocked fans by defeating Alabama 44–16. Lawrence passed for 347 yards and three touchdowns. He was the first freshman to lead his team to a national title in over 30 years.

During Lawrence's second season at Clemson, the Tigers once again went undefeated and made it all the way to the title game. But this time, they lost to Louisiana State University. The loss broke a 29-game winning streak for Lawrence and his team.

Lawrence had another great year in 2020. He threw for more than 3,000 yards and 24 touchdowns. But the Tigers lost in the playoffs to Ohio State.

SUPER SPORTS SCOOP

To help him bulk up in college, Lawrence ate two peanut butter and jelly sandwiches every day. He prefered crunchy peanut butter and strawberry jelly.

Though he did not win a second national title, Lawrence was one of the best young quarterbacks in the country. Some even compared him to NFL Hall of Famers such as John Elway and Peyton Manning. Lawrence was a finalist for the 2020 Heisman Trophy, the award for college football's best player. But the award ended up going to Alabama's DeVonta Smith.

Lawrence hands the ball to running back Travis Etienne in the 2019 College Football Playoff National Championship.

Lawrence holds his Jaguars jersey with wife Marissa Lawrence during the 2021 draft.

Lawrence had many personal and professional achievements in 2021. On April 10, he married his longtime girlfriend, Marissa Mowry. The pair had been dating since high school.

Just after his marriage, Lawrence entered the 2021 NFL Draft. The Jacksonville Jaguars selected Lawrence number one overall. That July, they offered him a four-year contract worth $36.8 million. The kid from Cartersville High had a new team to play for and a new title to chase.

CHAPTER 3

DIVISION CHAMP

Lawrence had some ups and downs in his rookie season. In his first NFL game, he threw for three touchdowns and three interceptions. Jacksonville opened the season with a five-game losing streak and finished the year 3–14.

But Lawrence had some strong games as well. His best game was the last of the year. He threw for 223 yards and two touchdowns in a 26–11 victory over the Indianapolis Colts.

The disappointing season prompted the Jaguars to fire their head coach. For the 2022 season, Jacksonville brought in a new head coach, Doug Pederson.

Lawrence and Jaguars coach Doug Pederson discuss a play during a game.

SUPER SPORTS SCOOP

Trevor Lawrence has worn uniform number 16 throughout his high school, college, and pro football careers. He chose 16 because he was a fan of Hall of Fame quarterback Peyton Manning, who wore 16 in college.

"It's been great getting to know him," Lawrence said before the start of the season. "There were a lot of changes we needed to make and I think he's made those."

At first, Pederson's changes didn't bring victories. Jacksonville started off the season 2–6. Some blamed the losses on Lawrence's play as quarterback. But Pederson stuck with Lawrence. Soon the rookie quarterback began leading the Jaguars to comeback wins, bringing their record to 8–8 with one game remaining.

The Jaguars still had a chance to win their division and make it into the playoffs. In the biggest game of his career, Lawrence completed 20 passes for 212 yards and a touchdown against the Tennessee Titans. The Jaguars won 20–16. For the first time since 2017, the team had earned the American Football Conference South Division title.

Lawrence passing the ball in a 2021 game against Tennessee

CHAPTER 4

NEXT STOP, SUPER BOWL?

After shocking the world by making the playoffs, the Jaguars surprised everyone again with their win over the Los Angeles Chargers. Most NFL experts had thought that Lawrence and the Jaguars would be no match for Chargers

In his second playoff game, Lawrence squared off with an even bigger opponent, Patrick Mahomes of the Kansas City Chiefs. In a battle of football's top young quarterbacks, Lawrence held his own. He completed 24 passes for 217 yards and a touchdown. But Mahomes was even better. The Chiefs won the game 27–20 and went on to win the Super Bowl.

Lawrence talks to Patrick Mahomes after the Jaguars lost to the Chiefs in the 2023 playoffs.

SUPER SPORTS SCOOP

Trevor Lawrence is close to his brother, Chase. Chase is an artist. The brothers worked together to create a series of football trading cards.

After the loss, Lawrence waited for his teammates as they walked off the field. He greeted each one to congratulate them on a successful season before heading to the locker room. He also had a message for all Jacksonville fans.

"Tough night," he tweeted after the game. "Thank you to everyone that was with us on this ride. We will be back." Ten days after the loss, Lawrence ended the season on a high when the NFL announced he had made the 2023 Pro Bowl.

With a playoff-tested team and a respected coach beside him, Trevor Lawrence should continue winning big games in future seasons. Could there be an MVP, or even a Super Bowl title, in his future? Only time will tell, but the possibilities are endless for one of pro football's best young quarterbacks.

Lawrence passes the ball in a 2023 game against the Kansas City Chiefs.

TREVOR LAWRENCE CAREER STATS

GAMES STARTED:

34

PASSES COMPLETED:

746

PASSES ATTEMPTED:

1,186

PASSING TOUCHDOWNS:

37

PASSING YARDS:

7,754

INTERCEPTIONS:

25

Stats are accurate through the 2022 NFL season.

GLOSSARY

conference: one of two groups of teams (the American Football Conference and the National Football Conference) in the NFL

draft: when teams take turns choosing new players

field goal: a score of three points in football made by kicking the ball over the crossbar

fumble: when a football player loses hold of the ball while handling or running with it

interception: a pass caught by the defending team

Most Valuable Player (MVP): an award given to the player who is considered the most valuable in the NFL

practice squad: a group of players that practices with the team but does not play in games

Pro Bowl: the NFL's all-star game

title: championship

touchdown: a scoring play worth six points

wide receiver: an offensive player whose main job is to catch passes

SOURCE NOTES

11 Grace Raynor, "The Tale of Trevor Lawrence: Small Town Hero Hits the Big Time at Clemson," *Charleston (SC) Post and Courier*, last modified September 14, 2020, https://www.postandcourier.com/sports/the-tale-of-trevor-lawrence-small-town-hero-hits-the-big-time-at-clemson/article_3112e41a-90f7-11e8-955a-67c4da654a1a.html.

22 Paul Kasabian, "Trevor Lawrence Discusses How HC Pederson Treats People after Playing for Urban Meyer," Bleacher Report, July 12, 2022, https://bleacherreport.com/articles/10041821-trevor-lawrence-discusses-how-hc-pederson-treats-people-after-playing-for-urban-meyer.

26 Mike McDaniel, "Trevor Lawrence Shares Promising Message after Jaguars' Loss to Chiefs," SI.com, January 21, 2023, https://www.si.com/nfl/2023/01/22/trevor-lawrence-shares-promising-message-after-jaguars-loss-to-chiefs.

LEARN MORE

Coleman, Ted. *Jacksonville Jaguars All-Time Greats*. Lake Elmo, MN: Press Room Books, 2022.

Doeden, Matt. *Meet Jalen Hurts*. Minneapolis: Lerner Publications, 2024.

Kiddle: American Football Facts for Kids
https://kids.kiddle.co/American_football

Lowe, Alexander. *G.O.A.T. Football Quarterbacks*. Minneapolis: Lerner Publications, 2023.

National Football League: Trevor Lawrence
https://www.nfl.com/players/trevor-lawrence/

Sports Illustrated Kids: Football
https://www.sikids.com/football

INDEX

PHOTO ACKNOWLEDGMENTS

Image credits: AP Photo/Greg Trott, p. 4; AP Photo/David Rosenblum/Icon Sportswire, p. 6; Kevin Sabitus/Getty Images, p. 7; Scott Cunningham/Getty Images, pp. 8, 9, 10, 12; Sean Gardner/Getty Images, p. 13; Chris Graythen/Getty Images, p. 14; C. Tilton/Getty Images, p. 15; Jordan Murph/Sports Illustrated/Getty Images, p. 16; Jamie Schwaberow/Getty Images, p. 18; AP Photo/Logan Bowles, p. 19; Carmen Mandato/Getty Images, p. 20; Mike Carlson/Getty Images, p. 21; Sam Greenwood/Getty Images, p. 23; Michael Allio/Icon Sportswire/Getty Images, p. 24; David Eulitt/Getty Images, p. 25; Cooper Neill/Getty Images, p. 27.

Cover: Kirby Lee/Alamy.